Pondering Tidbits of Truth

(Volume I)

Compiled and Edited by

Michael Seagriff

Pondering Tidbits of Truth

ISBN-13:978-0692210437
ISBN-10: 0692210431

Printed in the United States of America

Michael Seagriff
Canastota, New York

Dedication

To a loving God who shares His
wisdom by using flawed human
instruments, such as myself and those
men, women and organizations
represented by the timeless writings
and words quoted in this book.

Table of Contents

Introduction

We are all busy people. Many of us have convinced ourselves that we simply do not have the time to read, ponder and reflect on the wealth of spiritual wisdom our Catholic Church has accumulated over the centuries. Yet, we owe God and ourselves this reflective time.

If we spend little or no time pondering the truths and mysteries of our Faith, we are not going to progress spiritually - a growth essential to our eternal well-being and that of those around us.

More then two years ago, I started a bi-weekly column on my blog, Harvesting the Fruits of Contemplation, that I entitled *Pondering Tidbits of Truth*. It was then, and still remains, my simple and inadequate way of providing nuggets of spiritual wisdom for my readers to chew on from time to time. Rarely did these bi-weekly columns share a common thread.

Since these columns have turned out to be one of the more frequently visited and commented on portion of my blog, it was suggested I share them with a larger audience. That is the purpose of this little book.

You will find 100 quotations here. Some may be familiar to you. Others maybe not so much. All offer much fruit for your reflection and contemplation. I offer no apology for the frequent appearance of the Venerable Fulton J. Sheen – his clear and courageous voice is needed in our times.

This is my challenge to all who come upon this little book. Carry it with you or put it on your Kindle, tablet, laptop, android or I-phone so it will always be readily accessible at those times when you can steal a few minutes away from the hustle and demands of daily life to think about "what is above". Read these words and ponder them, asking God to let you understand what He wants you to learn from this material.

I suspect if you do as I have suggested, five things will happen: you will not tire of re-reading these truths from time to time; you will become hungry for additional spiritual nourishment; you will be eager to give

Our Lord even more of your time; you may even begin sharing with family and friends what you have learned – the fruits of your contemplation; and you will want to get a copy of my other book, *Forgotten Truths To Set Faith Afire! Words to Challenge, Inspire and Instruct* – at least I hope you will.

―――――――――――――

You can find my blog at:
http://harvestingthefruitsofcontemplation@blogspt.com/

(A peaceful picture to help you ponder the magnificence of He Who made you!)
(Photo©Michael Seagriff)

Quotations

[1]   Venerable Fulton J. Sheen

...in previous ages men lived in the sense of the Presence of God. As the earth carries its own atmosphere while it revolves around in space, so men carried with them their faith. Today, there is a feeling not of the Presence of God, but rather the absence of God: We have not lost our thirst, but we have denied the existence of water.

(Radicalism and Sacrifice)

[2]   *St. Augustine*

Too little does man love You who loves something together with You, loving it not because of You.

(The Confessions of St. Augustine)

[3]   St. John of the Cross

Endeavor to be inclined always: not to the easiest, but to the most difficult; not to the most delightful, but to the harshest; not to the most gratifying, but to the less pleasant; not to what means rest for you, but to hard work; not the consoling, but to the unconsoling; not to the most, but to the least; not to the highest and most precious, but to the lowest and most despised; not to wanting something, but to wanting nothing; do not go about looking for the best of temporal things, but for the worst and desire to enter for Christ into complete nudity, emptiness, and poverty in everything in the world. You should embrace these practices earnestly and try to overcome the repugnance of your will toward them. If you sincerely put them into practice, with order and discretion, you will discover in them, great delight and consolation...

(Ascent of Mount Carmel)

[4] *Madeleine Delbrel, Servant of God*

To the extent that our world tries to break itself away from God, that people believe that they can get by without God, that they can organize things apart from God, God becomes for the world something new, and the living God of the Gospel once again becomes news.

(*We, the Ordinary People of the Streets*)

[5] St. Teresa of Avila

The whole aim of any person who is beginning prayer – and don't forget this, because it is very important – should be that he work and prepare himself with determination and every effort to bring his will in conformity with God's will.

(*Interior Castle*)

[6] *St. Gregory the Great*

If people are scandalized at the Truth, it is better to allow the birth of scandal than to abandon the Truth.

(*Cited in Summa Theologiae II-II, Q43, Art 7*)

[7] Tertullian

We ourselves, though we're guilty of every sin, are not just a work of God; we're image. Yet we have cut ourselves off from our Creator in both soul and body. Did we get eyes to serve lust, the tongue to speak evil, ears to hear evil, a throat for gluttony, a stomach to be gluttony's ally, hands to do violence, genitals for unchaste excesses, feet for an erring life? Was the soul put in the body to think up traps, fraud and injustice? I don't think so.

(*On The Shows, 2*)

[8]   *Pope Francis*

Let the risen Jesus enter your life, welcome him as a friend, with trust: he is life! If up till now you have kept him at a distance, step forward. He will receive you with open arms. If you have been indifferent, take a risk: you won't be disappointed. If following him seems difficult, don't be afraid, trust him, be confident that he is close to you, he is with you and he will give you the peace you are looking for and the strength to live as he would have you do.

(*Easter Homily March 31, 2013*)

[9]   St. Pius X

Venerable Brethren, We must repeat with the utmost energy in these times of social and intellectual anarchy when everyone takes it upon himself to teach as a teacher and lawmaker - the City cannot be built otherwise than as God has built it; society cannot be setup unless the Church lays the foundations and supervises the work; no, civilization is not something yet to be found, nor is the New City to be built on hazy notions; it has been in existence and still is: it is Christian civilization, it is the Catholic City. It has only to be set up and restored continually against the unremitting attacks of insane dreamers, rebels and miscreants.

(*Notre Charge Apostolique*)

[10]   *St. Thomas Aquinas*

Man needs to know two things: the glory of God and the punishment of Hell. For through being drawn by His glory and terrified by His punishments, men are careful on their own account and refrain from sin.

(*Lenten Homilies 1274*)

[11]   Venerable Fulton Sheen

Sometimes the only way the good Lord can get into some hearts is to break them.

(Through The Year with Fulton Sheen)

[12]   *Jesus to St. Catherine of Siena*

Always keep your eyes on God. Let everything you do be directed toward God. Let each of you try to grow from strength to strength, never turning back to look at the world but keeping your heart constantly fixed on the thought of how short our time is. Ponder the price at which you have been so tenderly ransomed and the reward given to those who clothe themselves in virtue. In this way…you will grow more and more in holy desire. Then at the end of your life you will…come bound in love and charity, to that perfect union and vision of peace where there is joy and happiness completely free of sadness or bitterness.

(The Letters of St. Catherine of Siena, Vol. II, Suzanne Noffke, O.P., Tr.)

[13]   St. Augustine

Love of self till God is forgotten or love of God till self is forgotten.

(The City of God)

[14]   *Pope Emeritus Benedict XVI*

'What great nation is there, that has a god so near to it as the Lord our God is to us?' Let us beseech the Lord to reawaken in us the joy of his presence and that we may once more adore him. Without adoration, there is no transformation of the world.

(God Is Near Us)

[15]   Father Anthony J. Paone, S.J.

My child, human respect is the fear of being criticized or corrected by people. Live your life in My presence, and do not think too much of what people may think or say. As long as your conscience is clear, the thoughts or words of men can neither add to nor subtract from your true worth. You are not a better man when people praise you, nor are you worse when they find fault with you. You are what you are, and I see you as you really are. Your value in My eyes does not depend upon the judgments of people. I look upon your heart. I see your intentions and your sincere efforts. Men judge you mainly by your external actions. They cannot be sure of your merit or guilt in the deed. Too often they judge you by their own likes and dislikes, or by their own vanity and fixed ideas.

(My Daily Bread)

[16]   *St. Teresa of Avila*

The highest perfection consists not in interior favors or in great raptures but in the bringing of our wills so closely into conformity with the Will of God that, as soon as we realize that He wills anything, we desire it ourselves with all our might.

(Book of Foundations)

[17]   St. John Chrysostom

Let us submit to God in all things and not contradict Him, even if what He says seems contrary to our reason and intellect; rather, let His words prevail over our reason and intellect. Let us act in this way with regard to the (Eucharistic) mysteries, looking not only at what falls under our senses but holding on to His words. For His Word cannot lead us astray.

*(*Cited by Pope Paul VI *in Mysterium Fide)*

[18] *St. Pius X*

Most of the evils which beset the Church and most of the problems with which the Catholic Church is plagued, are not due to bad will. No, they are mainly due to ignorance of Christ's revealed truth.

(Acerbo Nimis, 1)

[19] Code of Canon Law

…The salvation of souls which must always be the supreme law in the Church, is to be kept before one's eyes.

(Code of Canon Law No. 1752)

[20] *Jesus to St. Catherine of Siena*

It [self-love] has poisoned the whole world and the mystical body of Holy Church and through it the garden of my spouse has run to seed and given birth to putrid flowers.

(The Dialogue)

[21] Venerable Fulton J. Sheen

…Christ affirms that when a man marries a woman, he marries both her body and her soul; he marries the whole person. If he gets tired of the body, he may not thrust her body away for another, since he is still responsible for her soul.

(The Life of Christ)

[22]   *St. Augustine*

We should hear the Gospel as if Our Lord were present and speaking to us. We must not say 'happy were those who could see him', for many of those who saw him crucified him; and many of those who have not seen him have believed in him. The very words that came from Our Lord's lips were written down and kept and preserved for us.

(Commentary on St. John's Gospel)

[23]   **Father Francis Fernandez**

If we do not place any obstacles in its way, if we allow it [the seed of grace] to grow, it will not fail to bear fruit. It does not depend on the person who does the sowing or the reaping: *God gives the growth*…Anyone who does not breathe dies of suffocation; anyone who does not accept with docility the grace that God constantly gives us ends by dying of spiritual suffocation.

(In Conversation With God, Vol 3.Section 23.1)

[24]   *Archbishop Charles. J. Chaput, O.F.M. Cap.*

For Pope Benedict, laypeople and priests don't need to publicly renounce their Catholic faith to be apostates; they simply need to be silent when their baptism demands that they speak out, to be cowards when Jesus asks them to have courage.

(The Role of the Priest in Public Affairs)

[25]   Father Paul Hinnesbusch, O.P.

But if the Real Presence of Christ in the Tabernacle is the sign and sacrament of the Lord in the midst of His People sending forth His saving power, Benediction signifies this even more impressively. It is the sign and sacrament of the Lord present among us, blessing us – distributing the wonderful fruits of His one all-suffering sacrifice, giving to each one according to his needs. You will recall that Pope John XXIII described a visit to the Blessed Sacrament as silent and adoring openness to receive these blessings, for the Lord Himself knows best our situation and what we need.

(The Real Presence, "It Is So!")

[26]   *Madeleine Delbrel, Servant of God*

The basic revelation of the Gospel is the overwhelming, penetrating presence of God. It is a call to encounter God, and God allows Himself to be encountered only in solitude.

(We, the Ordinary People of the Streets)

[27]   Cardinal Jorge Bergoglio (Pope Francis)

Rend your hearts to say with the Psalmist: "we have sinned." The wound of the soul is sin: Oh wounded poor recognize your doctor! Show him the wounds of your guilt. And since he is not hidden from our secret thoughts, let him feel the cry of your heart. Move it to compassion with your tears, your insistence! I hear your sighs, your pain so I reached, at last, to tell you: The Lord has put away your sin. This is the reality of our human condition. This is the truth that can approach genuine reconciliation with God and with men. This is not to discredit the self but to penetrate the depths of our heart and take care of the mystery of suffering and pain that binds us for centuries, for thousands of years, for always.

(Ash Wednesday Homily 2013)

[28]   *Pope Pius IX*

With God and Jesus Christ excluded from political life, with authority derived not from God, but from man, the very basis of that authority has been taken away, because the chief reason of the distinction between ruler and subject has been eliminated. The result is that human society is tottering to its fall, because it has no longer a secure and sound foundation.

(*The Companion to The Catechism of the Catholic Church: A Compendium of Texts Referred to in the Catechism of the Catholic Church*)

[29]   Blessed Cardinal John Henry Newman

Nothing would be done at all, if we waited until one could do it so well that no one could find fault with it.

(Lectures on the Present Position of Catholics in England (1851)

[30] *Venerable Fulton J. Sheen*

Christian love bears evil, but it does not tolerate it. It does penance for the sins of others, but it is not broadminded about sin. REAL LOVE involves real hatred: whoever has lost the power of moral indignation and the urge to drive the sellers from the temple has also lost a living, fervent love of Truth.

(Love Is Not Tolerance)

[31] St. Teresa of Avila

If anyone advises you to give up your prayer, take no notice of him. You may be sure he is a false prophet.

(The Way of Perfection)

[32] *The Congregation For Clergy*

Whenever a confessor is available, sooner or later a penitent will arrive. And if the confessor continues to make himself available, even stubbornly so, sooner or later many penitents will arrive! Our rediscovery of the Sacrament of Reconciliation, both as penitents and as ministers, is a measure of authentic faith in the saving action of God which shows itself more clearly in the power of grace than in human strategic or pastoral initiatives which sometimes overlook this essential truth.

(The Priest Minister of Divine Mercy: An Aid for Confessors and Spiritual Directors)

[33] St. Catherine of Siena

For nails would not have held God-and-Man fast to the cross, had love not held Him there.

(What Have The Saints to Teach Us)

[34]   Venerable Fulton J. Sheen

Judas Iscariot is the patron saint of social justice - where people are concerned with humanity, but ignore the truths of God.

(For Life and Family blogspot.com/)

[35]   St. John Marie Vianney

We can very well say that the Passion which the Jews made Christ suffer was almost nothing compared with what Christians make him undergo with their insults of mortal sins…what horror there will be when Jesus Christ shows us the things for which we have abandoned Him!

(Sermon on Sin)

[36]   *Blessed Cardinal John Henry Newman*

The Catholic Church holds it better for the sun and moon to drop from heaven, for the earth to fail, and for all the many millions on it to die of starvation in extreme agony, as far as temporal affliction goes, than that one soul, I will not say, should be lost, but should commit one single venial sin, should tell one willful untruth, or should steal one poor farthing without excuse.

(Apologia Pro Vita Sua)

[37]   Rafael Cardinal Merry del Val

Have a great devotion to the Passion of Our Lord. With peace and resignation, put up with your daily troubles and worries. Remember that you are not a disciple of Christ unless you partake of His sufferings and are associated with His Passion. The help of the grace of silence was the only thing that enabled the saints to carry their extremely heavy crosses. We can show our love for Him by accepting with joy the cross He sends our way.

(The Power of the Cross- Applying The Passion of Christ to Your Life by Michael Dubriel)

[38] *Venerable Fulton J. Sheen*

Poor in spirit [referenced in the Sermon on the Mount]...does not mean indigent. To be poor in spirit is to be conscious of one's spiritual poverty, to blush at one's own defects, to have a deep sense of nothingness before God, and to be resigned before the beneficent Hand of Providence. The foundation of all spiritual happiness is to be conscious before God of one's emptiness or one's need, like the publican smiting his breast. Poverty of spirit is the very antithesis of the worldly doctrine of self-sufficiency.

(The Life of Christ)

[39] **Dr. Ralph Martin**

The reason for the command [for example in Matthew 28:18-20 and Acts 1:8] – namely, that the eternal destinies of human beings are really at stake and for most people the preaching of the Gospel can make a life-or-death, heaven or hell difference – need to be unashamedly stated. This is certainly why Jesus often spoke of the eternal consequences of not accepting his teaching – being lost forever, hell – and did not just give the command to evangelize. This is why Mark 16:16, which is referenced in LG [*Lumen Gentium 16*] but not directly quoted, makes explicit that what is at stake is being "saved" or "condemned." Jesus makes clear that Christianity is not a game or an optional enrichment opportunity but a precious and urgent opportunity to find salvation and escape damnation. In fidelity to the teaching of Christ this is what motivated two thousand years of heroic missionary work and the heroic witness of countless martyrs.

(*Will Many Be Saved? What Vatican II Actually Teaches and Its Implications for The New Evangelization*)

[40] *Pope Emeritus Benedict XVI*

Jesus came to tell us everyone is wanted in paradise, and that hell, about which little gets said today, exists and is eternal for those who close their hearts to His love.

(*Homily* March 25, 2007)

[41] Judge Robert H. Bork

Those of us used to the soft, therapeutic religions of the present day forget how rigorous religion used to be, Protestant as well as Catholic. As life became easier and diversions more plentiful, men are less willing to accept the authority of their clergy and less willing to worship a demanding God, a God who dictates how one should live and puts a great many bodily and psychological pleasures off limits.

(*Slouching Towards Gomorrah: Modern Liberalism and American Decline*)

[42] *Father Anthony J. Paone, S.J.*

[Jesus speaking:]
Forget yourself and you will forget someone far greater - Me. Let Me decide what your life shall be each day. No offering of yours can please Me completely until you have given Me the greatest gift of all - your will. Do this by preferring whatever I send you each day. Do your very best, and then accept the results as My will.

(*My Daily Bread*)

[43] Venerable Fulton J. Sheen

Is it the business of Christ to win followers by elaborate social programs? This is one form of life. Or is it the business of Christ to be willing to love all the stomach-minded at the cost of reaching the few with faith, to whom will be given the Bread of Life and the wine that germinates virgins?

(*Life Of Christ (188)*

13

[44]   *St. Catherine of Siena*

[Jesus speaking:] "I distribute the virtues quite diversely; I do not give all of them to each person...I shall give principally charity to one; justice to another; humility to this one; a living faith to that one...And so, I have given many gifts and graces, both spiritual and temporal, with such diversity that I have not given everything to one single person, so that you may be constrained to practice charity towards one another.

(Catechism of the Catholic Church 1937)

[45]   **Pope Paul VI**

The most sacred task of theology is not the invention of new dogmatic formulas to replace old ones, but rather such a defense and explanation of the formulas adopted by the councils as may demonstrate that divine revelation is the source of the truths communicated through those expressions.

(Encyclical Mysterium Fidei - Mystery of Faith)

[46]   *Peter J. Leithart*

If the Church of the martyrs has one thing to teach us, it is this: The Church is most politically potent not when she has a place in the halls of power, but when she shares the testimony of Jesus regardless of the consequences.

(Witness Unto Death published in First Things January 2013)

[47] St. Cyprian

Our obligation is to do God's will, and not our own. We must remember this if the prayer that our Lord commanded us to say daily is to have any meaning on our lips. How unreasonable it is to pray that God's will be done, and then not promptly obey it when he calls us from this world! Instead we struggle and resist like self-willed slaves and are brought into the Lord's presence with sorrow and lamentation, not freely consenting to our departure, but constrained by necessity. And yet we expect to be rewarded with heavenly honors by him to whom we come against our will! Why then do we pray for the kingdom of heaven to come if this earthly bondage pleases us? What is the point of praying so often for its early arrival if we would rather serve the devil here than reign with Christ?

The world hates Christians, so why give your love to it instead of following Christ, who loves you and has redeemed you?...Our part, our dear brothers, is to be single-minded, firm in faith, and steadfast in courage, ready for God's will, whatever it may be. Banish the fear of death and think of the eternal life that follows it...

(*Sermon on Man's Mortality*, Office of Readings)

[48] *Father Alfred Delp, S.J.*

Bread is important, freedom is more important, but most important of all is unbroken fidelity and faithful adoration.

(Quoted by Pope Benedict XVI in *Jesus of Nazareth*)

[49]   Venerable Fulton J. Sheen

Very few today believe in the devil. This is exactly what the devil wants. He is always circulating the news of his death. The essence of God is existence, and He defines Himself as: 'I am Who am.' The essence of the devil is the lie, and he defines himself as: 'I am who am not.' Satan never has to bother with those who do not believe in him; they are already his. But he has a lot of trouble with the saints who are constantly and literally sending him to hell. Satan keeps thousands of devils stationed on monastery walls, but only one in a large city. There are probably some places where the devil sleeps, because he has no work to do. The devil has used many in our western world to convince us that there is no hell – a thing rather hard to believe, when there is so much evidence for hell around us…

(*The Life of Christ*)

[50]   *Saint John of Kronstadt*

What would happen, O my Lord God, Jesus Christ, if You made the light of Your divinity to shine from Your most Holy Sacrament, when the priest brings It in his hands to a sick person? Before this light, all who would encounter It or see It would fall prostrate on the ground spontaneously, just as the angels cover their faces before this Sacrament. While on the other hand, so many treat this heavenly Sacrament with indifference.

(*Dominus Est - It Is The Lord!* by Most Rev. Athanasius Schneider)

[51]   St. Peter Julian Eymard

It is impossible for anyone to bestow upon us a love for Jesus Christ or infuse it into our hearts. People may exhort us to love Him, but it is beyond human power for us to teach how to love; we learn love by feeling it. This education of the heart belongs to our Lord alone, for He desires Himself alone to be its goal. He begins by giving to the communicant the sentiment of love, then the motive of love, and finally the impelling desire for the heroism of love. But this is learned only in Communion.

(How To Get More Out of Holy Communion)

[52]   *Blessed Columba Marmion, O.S.B.*

Never forget this truth: the Eternal Father is pleased with us only in so far as we imitate His Son and inasmuch as He sees in us the likeness of His Son, for it is in His image that He has predestined us from all eternity. For us there is no other form of sanctity than that which Christ has shown us. The degree of our perfection is measured by the degree of our imitation of Jesus and of our union with Him.

(The Mysteries of the Rosary)

[53]   Venerable Fulton J. Sheen

The Sermon on the Mount is so much at variance with all that our world holds dear, that the world will crucify anyone who strives to live up to its values; because Christ preached them, he had to die. Calvary was the price He paid for the Sermon on the Mount. Only mediocrity survives. Those who call black, black and white, white are sentenced for intolerance. Only the grays live.

(The Life of Christ)

[54]   Pope Emeritus Benedict XVI

Today…it is particularly important to clarify the criteria used to distinguish the authentic sensus fidelium from its counterfeits. In fact, it is not some kind of public opinion of the Church, and it is unthinkable to mention it in order to challenge the teachings of the Magisterium, this because the sensus fidei cannot grow authentically in the believer except to the extent in which he or she fully participates in the life of the Church, and this requires a responsible adherence to her Magisterium.

(Address to the International Theological Commission, December 7, 2012)

[55]   Dr. Ralph Martin

How tragic if the promulgation of a theoretical or practical presumption that almost everyone will be saved actually became the cause of many people being lost.

(Will Many Be Saved? What Vatican II Actually Teaches and Its Implications for The New Evangelization)

[56]   *Madeleine Delbrel, Servant of God*

To take the Word of God seriously, we need all the strength of the Holy Spirit. If our witness is often mediocre, it is because we have not realized that the same kind of heroism is needed to be a witness as to be a martyr.

(We, the Ordinary People of the Streets)

[57]   Father Winfrid Herbst, S.D.S.

I am sure many lost souls in hell right now would cry out to preachers and writers if they could: Oh, why did you not tell us more about the horrors of hell? Why did you not strike such fear into our hearts by your realistic description of hell that we would have made greater efforts to avoid it?...Why did you spare our feelings in a matter of such eternal moment? Oh, why did you not make hell a thousand times hotter than you did, then perhaps we would not be here today?

(The Way To God)

[58]   *Venerable Fulton J. Sheen*

A prophet is a Divine Troubler, not a political troubler. He is always a disturber of worldly peace; he makes listeners feel uneasy.

(Divine Troubler by Carl E. Olson, *Our Sunday Visitor*, October 3, 2013)

[59]   Mike Aquilina

How much of my effort goes into securing prosperity and peace for myself and my family? How much of my effort goes into securing heaven for us?

(A Year with the Church Fathers)

[60]   *St. Alphonsus Liguori*

God is ready to heal those who sincerely wish to amend their lives, but cannot take pity on the obstinate sinner. The Lord pardons sins, but he cannot pardon those who are determined to offend Him. He who receives pardon is pardoned through the pure mercy of God, and they who are chastised, are justly punished. But, God is not obliged to wait for your repentance.

(A Sermon On The Number of Sins Beyond Which God Pardons No More)

[61]   Venerable Fulton J. Sheen

All men are born to live; He (Jesus) was born to do the Father's business which was to die and thereby save."

(Life of Christ)

[62]   *Catherine de Heuck Doherty, Servant of God*

We don't need psychiatrists for our priests. We don't need counselors for our priests. We need priests to take us by the hand and lead us to sanctity.

*(*Audio Conference - *Discerning Hearts)*

[63]   St. Pius X

In our time more than ever before, the chief strength of the wicked, lies in the cowardice and weakness of good men. All the strength of Satan's reign is due to the easy-going weakness of Catholics.

Oh! If I might ask the Divine Redeemer, as the prophet Zachary did in spirit: What are those wounds in the midst of Thy hands? The answer would not be doubtful: With these I was wounded in the house of them that loved Me. I was wounded by My friends, who did nothing to defend Me and, who on every occasion, made themselves the accomplices of my adversaries. And this reproach can be leveled against the weak and timid Catholics of all countries.

(Discourse at the Beatification of St. Joan of Arc, Dec. 13, 1908)

[64]   Venerable Fulton J. Sheen

God could never let you suffer a pain or a reversal or experience sadness if it could not in some way minister to your perfection. If he did not spare his own Son on the Cross for the redemption of the world, then you may be sure that he will sometimes not spare your wants that you might be all you need to be: happy and perfect children of a loving Father. He may even permit us to wage wars as a result of our selfishness that we may learn there is no peace except in Goodness and Truth.

(*Daily Readings in Catholic Classics*)

[65]   Madeleine Delbrel, Servant of God

Once we have heard God's Word, we no longer have the right not to accept it; once we have accepted it, we no longer have the right not to let it become flesh in us; once it has become flesh in us, we no longer have the right to keep it for ourselves alone. Henceforward, we belong to all those who are waiting for the Word.

(We, *the Ordinary People of the Streets*)

[66]   *Sister Josefa Menendez*

I saw several souls fall into Hell, and among them a child of fifteen, cursing her parents for not having taught her to fear God, and that Hell actually exits.

(*The Way of Divine Love*)

[67]   Anne Costa

There are no unforgivable sins, only unconfessed ones, and there are no sins greater than God's mercy.

(*Lord, I Hurt!*)

[68]   *Venerable Fulton J. Sheen*

Every worldly priest hinders the growth of the Church; every saintly priest promotes it. If only all priests realized how their holiness makes the Church holy, and how the Church begins to decline as the level of holiness among priests falls below that of the people!

(The Priest Is Not His Own)

[69]   **Blessed Pier Giorgio Frassati**

We who, by the grace of God, are Catholics, must not squander the best years of our lives as so many unhappy young people do, who worry about enjoying the good things in life, things that do not in fact bring any good, but rather the fruit of immorality in today's world. We must prepare ourselves to be ready and able to handle the struggles we will have to endure to fulfill our goals, and, in so doing, to give our country happier and morally healthier days in the near future. But in order for this to happen we need the following: constant prayer to obtain God's grace, without which all our efforts are in vain; organization and discipline to be ready for action at the right moment; and finally, we need to sacrifice our own passions, indeed our very selves, because without this sacrifice we will never achieve goal.

(From Blessed Pier Giorgio Frassati: An Ordinary Christian)

[70]   *Blessed Teresa of Calcutta*

If you are discouraged it is a sign of pride because it shows you trust in your own power. Your self-sufficiency, your selfishness and your intellectual pride will inhibit His coming to live in your heart because God cannot fill what is already full. It is as simple as that.

(7 Steps To A Holier Life)

[71]   Leo Rudloff, O.S.B.

The existence of hell brings home to us with terrifying clarity the fact that God is just, and that His justice is not to be separated from His mercy. We must stress with special emphasis, however, that hell is not a blind destiny into which the sinner plunges unawares, but is his self-chosen and fully deserved portion.

(Everyman's Theology)

[72]   *St. Teresa of Avila*

St. Theresa of Avila once heard someone say: "If only I had lived at the time of Jesus... If only I had seen Jesus...If only I had talked with Jesus"...To this, St. Theresa replied: "But do we not have in the Eucharist the living, true and real Jesus present before us? Why look for Him?"

(Author Unknown)

[73]   Pope Paul VI

[The Church] exists in order to evangelize, that is to say, in order to preach and teach, to be the channel of the gift of grace, to reconcile sinners with God, and to perpetuate Christ's sacrifice in the Mass, which is the memorial of His death and glorious resurrection.

(Evangelii Nuntiandi)

[74]   *St. Thomas Aquinas*

Man should not consider his material possessions his own, but as common to all, so as to share them without hesitation when others are in need.

(Church and State Through the Centuries)

[75]   Venerable Fulton J. Sheen

Each morning we priests hold in our hands the Christ, who shed blood from His veins, tears from His eyes, sweat from His body to sanctify us. How we should be on fire with that love, that we may enkindle it in others.

(The Priest is Not His Own)

[76]   *Father Giovanni Salerno*

For Missionary Servants of the Poor it is a great privilege to represent the Church and the Holy Father in the midst of the poor. When the missions of the Third World are spoken of, many think that the best way to help the poor is to address their material needs: clothing, medicine, food, etc. In my life as missionary, after forty-six years, I have realized that the greatest gift we can give the poor is God and His divine grace through the Sacraments of the Church.

(Letter to Abbot at Our Lady of Clear Creek Abbey)

[77]   Madeleine Delbrel, Servant of God

Saving the world does not mean making it happy; it means showing the world the meaning of its suffering and giving it a joy that "nothing can take away." If we must fight against the misery and misfortune which Christ took so seriously as to speak of judging us in the end solely by what we did for others in this regard, we must keep in mind that what is at stake is ultimately not solving these problems and constructing a second earthly paradise; rather, what is at stake is eternal life.

(We the Ordinary People of the Streets)

[78] *Father Reginald Garrigou-Lagrange, O.P.*

The primary purpose of the priestly grace is the worthy celebration of the Sacrifice of the Mass…The secondary purpose of the grace which the priest receives at ordination is the sanctification of the faithful. If the priest has the care of souls, he has a special obligation to strive for holiness of life because of his duty toward the Mystical Body of Christ. In no other way will he be able to sanctify the souls committed to his charge or avoid the dangers of the world…

(*The Priest In Union With Christ*)

[79] **Father Walter Farrell, O.P.**

There is no man God does not wish to be saved; but there is no man God will save against that man's will. It would be a poor kind of love that made us in His image and left us nothing to do for ourselves; it is a Divine love that sets out a man's work for a man's life and stands by a man's own decisions. He has indeed left us something to do with our mind and our will as well as with our hands and our feet. If we do these things, we are fulfilling the divine will; if we do not, we are not thwarting God but ourselves, for our eternal happiness hangs on the condition of our activity This is not a reason for despair; rather it is a divine tribute to the nobility of the nature of man.

(*My Way of Life*)

[80] *St. John Eudes*

Our wish, our object, our chief preoccupation must be to form Jesus in ourselves, to make His spirit, His devotion, His affections, His desires and His disposition live and reign there. All our religious exercises should be directed to this end. It is the work which God has given us to do unceasingly.

(*The Life and Reign of Jesus in Christian Souls*)

[81]   Venerable Fulton J. Sheen

The pastor's primary concern should be the tabernacle, not the rectory, not the ego, but the Lord, not his comfort, but God's glory.

(The Priest Is Not His Own)

[82]   *Thomas Dubay, S.M.*

In the view of St. Teresa of Avila and of St. John of the Cross, many think they are "listening to the Spirit", whereas in fact they are hearing nothing other than their own ideas and desires. They baptize their own preferences and somehow convince themselves, at times others as well, that they enjoy a privileged access to the divine.

(Fire Within)

[83]   St. Catherine of Siena

We've had enough of exhortations to be silent! Cry out with a hundred thousand tongues. I see that the world is rotten because of silence.

(Source unknown)

[84]   *Father Frederick Faber*

If we hated sin as we ought to hate it, purely, keenly, manfully, we should do more penance, we should inflict more self-punishment, we should sorrow for our sins more abidingly. Then, again, the crowning disloyalty to God is heresy. It is the sin of sins, the very loathsomest of things which God looks down upon in this malignant world. Yet how little do we understand of its excessive hatefulness! It is the polluting of God's truth, which is the worst of all impurities.
Yet how light we make of it! We look at it and are calm. We touch it and do not shudder. We mix with it and have no fear. We see it touch holy things, and we have no sense of sacrilege. We breathe its odor, and show no signs of detestation or disgust. Some of us affect its friendship; and some even extenuate its guilt. We do not love God enough to be angry for His glory. We do not love men enough to be charitably truthful for their souls.

(The Precious Blood)

[85] St. Teresa of Avila

It is quite certain that, when we empty ourselves of all that is creature and rid ourselves of it for the love of God, that same Lord will fill our souls with Himself.

(Interior Castle)

[86] *Madeleine Delbrel, Servant of God*

From a sand dune, dressed in white, the missionary overlooks an expanse of lands filled with unbaptized peoples. From the top of a long subway staircase, dressed in an ordinary suit or overcoat, we overlook, on each step, during this busy rush-hour time, an expanse of heads, of bustling heads, waiting for the door to open. Caps, berets, hats and hair of every color. Hundreds of heads – hundreds of souls. And there we stand, above. And above us, and everywhere is God. God is everywhere – and how many souls even take notice.

(We, the Ordinary People of the Street)

[87] Venerable Fulton J. Sheen

He [Jesus] refused to lead any revolutionary movement even among a conquered people and His own people. At no time did He take a stand in the quarrel between Herod and Pilate, or against the numerous political scandals that were so rampant in Judea. He never raises his voice against crucifixions, which he knew well as a boy when 3000 were crucified in the town easily visible from Nazareth. He was indifferent to power, except to affirm that all power comes from God.

(Those Mysterious Priests)

[88] *St. Claude de la Colombiere, S.J.*

Imagine the anguish and tears of a mother who is present at a painful operation her child has to undergo. Can anyone doubt on seeing her that she consents to allow the child to suffer only because she expects it to get well and be spared further suffering by means of this violent remedy?

Reason in the same manner when adversity befalls you. You complain that you are ill-treated, insulted, slandered, robbed. Your Redeemer (the name is a tenderer one than that of father or mother), your Redeemer is a witness to all you are suffering. He who loves you and has emphatically declared that whoever touches you touches the apple of His eye, nevertheless allows you to be stricken though He could easily prevent it. Do you hesitate to believe that this passing trial is necessary for the health of your soul?

(Trustful Surrender To Divine Providence)

[89] Pope Emeritus Benedict XVI

How do I treat God's Holy name? Do I stand in reverence before the mystery of the burning bush, before His incomprehensible closeness, even to the point of His presence in the Eucharist, where He truly gives Himself entirely into our hands? Do I take care that God's holy companionship with us will draw us up into His purity and sanctity, instead of dragging Him down into the filth?

(Jesus of Nazareth)

[90] *St. Edmund Campion*

[When asked to save his life by renouncing his Catholic Faith, this saint had this to say;] Your Majesty, for the past ten years I have given this matter thought. I thought about it seriously when I left the Church of England and went to the continent to be reconciled with Rome. I thought of it seriously when I entered the Society of Jesus and was ordained a priest. And ever since I have been back in England, how many times I thought that I could indeed save my life if I turned traitor to my Lord Christ and His Church! But He Himself has said to us all: 'He who would save his life must lose it.' I remain true to Christ and His Church.

(Edmund Campion-Hero of God's Underground by Harold C. Gardiner, S.J)

[91] Jean-Baptiste Chautard, O.C.S.O.

It is impossible to meditate upon the consequences of the dogma of the Real Presence, of the Sacrifice of the Altar, and of Communion without being led to the conclusion that Our Lord wanted to institute this Sacrament in order to make it the center of all action, of all loyal idealism, of every apostolate that could be of any real use to the Church.

(The Soul of the Apostolate)

[92] *Pope Francis*

Paul is a nuisance; he is a man, who with his preaching, his work, his attitude, irritates others, because testifying to Jesus Christ and the proclamation of Jesus Christ makes us uncomfortable, it threatens our comfort zones – even Christian comfort zones, right? It irritates us. The Lord always wants us to move forward, forward, forward – not to take refuge in a quiet life, or in cozy structures, no? And Paul, in preaching of the Lord, was a nuisance. But he had deep within him that most Christian of attitudes: Apostolic zeal.

(Homily, May 16, 2013)

[93] Venerable Fulton J. Sheen

Moral principles do not depend on a majority vote. Wrong is wrong, even if everybody is wrong. Right is right, even if no nobody is right.

(1953)

[94] *Bishop Pierre Camus*

The one point on which he [St. Francis de Sales] chiefly insisted was that "we must fear God from love, not love God from fear." Come beloved child, come near to the Heart that loves you so and LISTEN...LISTEN...because love's perfection consists in listening, more than in speaking...in working more than feeling.

(Holy Hours by Concepcion Cabrera de Armida

[95] St. Vincent Ferrer

Do you desire to study to your advantage? Let devotion accompany your studies, and study less to make yourself learned than to become a saint. Consult God more than books, and ask Him, with humility, to make you understand what you read. Study fatigues and drains the mind and heart. Go from time to time to refresh them at the feet of Jesus Christ under His cross. Some moments of repose in His Sacred Wounds give fresh vigor and new lights. Interrupt your application by short but fervent and ejaculatory prayers; never begin or end your study but by prayer.

(From St. Vincent Ferrer, Confessor (1350-1419)
http://www.ewtn.com/library/mary/ferrer.htm)

[96] *St. Catherine of Siena*

I distribute the virtues quite diversely; I do not give all of them to each person...I shall give principally charity to one; justice to another; humility to this one; a living faith to that one...And so, I have given many gifts and graces, both spiritual and temporal, with such diversity that I have not given everything to one single person, so that you may be constrained to practice charity towards one another.

(Catechism of the Catholic Church 1937)

[97] St. Teresa of Avila

I have been quite alarmed to find how possible it is for people to think that they see what they do not.

(The Book of The Foundations)

[98] *Father Paul Hinnesbusch, O.P.*

...any Tabernacle where Christ is present is the spiritual center of the whole Church and of all mankind, because He who is really here is upholding His living members everywhere by His spiritual power. But His Real Presence in the Tabernacle is the tangible sign that He is in the midst of His People. The Blessed Sacrament in the Tabernacle gives a living sense of this Presence.

(The Real Presence, "It Is So!")

[99] **Father Simon Tugwell, O.P.**

Faith punctures the self-sufficiency of our world, so that there is room for God to be God. Perfect charity is when that puncture has become all-embracing, so that we are nothing but space for God to be God.

(Magnificat - Year of Faith Companion)

[100] *Blaise Pascal*

There are only three types of people; those who have found God and serve him; those who have not found God and seek him, and those who live not seeking, or finding him. The first are rational and happy; the second unhappy and rational, and the third foolish and unhappy.

(Pensees)

Individuals Quoted
(Page references are within parenthesis)

Mike Aquilina contemporary Catholic author and occasional EWTN host (19)

Thomas Aquinas (Saint) (1225-1274) Italian Dominican priest, philosopher, theologian, Doctor of the Church (3, 23)

Augustine (Saint) (354-430) Bishop of Hippo, philosopher, theologian and writer (1, 4, 7)

Benedict XVI (Pope Emeritus) German priest, professor, theologian, author, Cardinal and only second Pope to resign (4, 13, 18, 28)

Robert H. Bork (Judge) (1927-2012) Author, conservative jurist, legal scholar, and Catholic convert (13)

Edmund Campion (Father, S.J.) (1540-1581) Jesuit priest and martyr (28)

Pierre Camus (Bishop) (1584-1652) Gifted preacher and close friend of St. Francis de Sales (29)

Catherine of Siena (Saint) (1347-1380) Lay tertiary of the Dominican Order, mystic, Doctor of the Church, one of the two patron saints of Italy (4, 6, 10, 14, 26, 30)

Archbishop Charles J. Chaput, O.F.M, Cap. (current Archbishop of Philadelphia (7)

Jean-Baptiste Chautard, O.C.S.O. (1858-1935) Trappist Abbot and author, whose book "The Soul of the Apostolate", was valued by St. Pius X and Pope Benedict XV (29)

John Chrysostom (Saint) (344-407) Eloquent preacher, theologian, liturgist, Archbishop of Constantinople, and a Doctor of the Church (5)

Congregation For The Clergy (10)

Anne Costa contemporary Christian author and speaker whose published works include *Refresh Me Lord!* and *Lord, I Hurt!* (21)

Cyprian (Saint) 3rd century Bishop of Carthage and martyr (15)

Code of Canon Law (6)

Claude de la Colombiere (Saint) (1641-1682) Jesuit priest, confessor to St. Margaret Mary Alacoque, and zealous apostle of the devotion to the Sacred Heart of Jesus (28)

Madeleine Delbrel (Servant of God) (1904-1964) French Catholic author, poet and mystic (2, 8, 18, 21, 24, 27)

Alfred Delp (Father, S.J.) (1907-1945) German Jesuit priest who was imprisoned and later executed for his opposition to Nazis. Some of his incarceration reflections have been published in a book entitled *The Prison Writings* (15)

Catherine de Heuck Doherty (Servant of God) (1896-1985) Russian immigrant, social justice activist, and foundress of Madonna House Apostolate (20)

Thomas Dubay (Father, S.M.) (1922-2010) Marist priest, teacher of seminarians, retreat master and an expert on the writings and teachings of St. John of the Cross and St. Teresa of Avila (26)

John Eudes (Saint) (1601-1680) French missionary priest, founder of two religious orders (Congregation of Jesus and Mary and the Sisters of Our Lady of Charity) (25)

Peter Julian Eymard (Saint) (1811-1839) French Catholic priest, an Apostle of the Eucharist, and founder of two religious orders, the Congregation of the Blessed Sacrament and the Servants of the Blessed Sacrament (17)

Frederick Faber (Father) (1814-1863) An English Catholic convert, priest, theologian and writer of hymns (7, 26)

Walter Farrell, S.T.M. (Father O.P.) (1902-1951) Dominican preacher, theologian and author (25)

Francis Fernandez (Father) Spanish priest, author and member of *Opus Dei* who was born in 1938 (7)

Vincent Ferrer, O.P. (Saint) (1350-1419) Dominican preacher and missionary through Europe, whose sermons on The Last Four Things resulted in thousands of Jews, Muslims and lapsed Catholics accepting and/or returning to the Catholic Faith (30)

Pier Giorgio Frassati (Blessed) (1901-1925) Lay Dominican, social activist and servant to the poor and sick (22)

Reginald Garrigou-Lagrange (Father, O.P.) (1877-1964) French Dominican priest, theologian, lecturer and author (25)

Gregory the Great (Pope) (Saint) (540-604) Doctor of the Church, prolific writer, reigned from 590 to 604 (2)

Winfrid Herbst, (Father S.D.S.) (1891-1998) Salvatorian priest and spiritual writer (19)

Paul Hinnesbusch (Father, O.P.) (1917-2002) Dominican priest, theologian, teacher, lecturer, chaplain and author (8, 31)

John of the Cross (Saint) (1542-1591) Spanish mystic, Carmelite friar, priest, and spiritual writer (1)

John Kronstadt (Saint) Russian Orthodox priest (16)

Peter J. Leithart Contemporary Christian author and theologian (14)

Alphonsus Liguori, (Saint) (1698-1787) Italian Bishop, spiritual writer, theologian, and founder of the Redemptorists (19)

Columba Marmion, O.S.B. (Blesssed) (1858-1923) Irish Benedictine monk, Abbot, and extraordinary spiritual author (17)

Ralph Martin (Dr.) contemporary Catholic author, president of Renewal Ministries and faculty member at Sacred Heart Major Seminary (12, 18)

Josefa Menendez (Sister) (1890-1923) Spanish mystic who joined the Order of the Sacred Heart of Jesus in France (21)

Rafael Cardinal Merry del Val (Servant of God) (1865-1930) Secretary of State for Pope St. Pius X (11)

John Henry Cardinal Newman (Blessed) (1801-1890) Anglican convert to Catholicism, author and Cardinal (9, 11)

Anthony J. Paone (Father, S.J.) Jesuit priest and in1954 authored *My Daily Bread* (5, 13)

Paul VI (Pope) (1897-1978) reigned as Pope from June 21, 1963 through August 6, 1978. Issued the Encyclical *Humanae Vitae* (14, 23)

Blaise Pascal (1623-1662) French inventor, mathematician, writer and Christian philosopher (31)

Pius IX (Blessed) (1792-1878) His was the longest pontificate in Church history. He was staunch opponent of false liberalism and convened the First Vatican Council (9)

Pius X (Saint) (1835-1914) succeeded Leo XIII and served from 1903 to 1914 (3, 6, 20)

Pope Francis (formerly Cardinal Jorge Bergoglio) our current Pope (3, 9, 29)

Leo Rudloff (Father O.S.B.) (1902-1982) Author, founder and first Abbot of Weston Priory in Weston, Vermont (23)

Giovanni Salerno (Father) contemporary missionary priest and founder of the Missionary Servants of the Poor (24)

Fulton Sheen (Servant of God) (1895-1979) Archbishop, renowned theologian, prolific writer and best known television and radio evangelist of his time (1, 4, 6, 10, 11, 12, 13, 16, 17, 19, 20, 21, 22, 24, 26, 27, 29)

Teresa of Avila (Saint) (1515-1582) Reformer of the Carmelite Order, Doctor of the Church and spiritual writer (2, 5, 10, 27, 30)

Teresa of Calcutta (Blessed) (1910-1997) Founder of the Missionary Sisters of Charity. Nobel Peace Prize winner (22)

Tertullian (160-220) early Church writer (12)

Simon Tugwell (Father, O.P.) English Dominican priest and author (31)

John Vianney (Saint) (1786-1859) Patron saint of all priests, known Cure of Ars (11)

Suggested Reading

This is a listing of books and articles referenced herein which you may wish to read in their entirety:

Aquilina, Mike. *A Year with the Church Fathers*. Charlotte, NC: St. Benedict Press. 2010

Augustine. *The City of God*. Peabody, MA: Henrickson Publishers, Inc. 2009

Benedict XVI Pope Emeritus. *God Is Near Us*. San Francisco. CA: Ignatius Press. 2003

Benedict XVI. Pope Emeritus. *Jesus of Nazareth*. New York, NY: Doubleday. 2007

Bork, Robert H. *Slouching Towards Gomorrah: Modern Liberalism and American Decline*. New York, NY: Regan Books/Harper Collins Publishers, Inc. 1997

Catherine of Siena. (Saint) Translator: Algar Thorold. *The Dialogue of St. Catherine of Siena*. Rockford, IL: Tan Books and Publishers, Inc. 1974

Chaput, Charles J. O.F.M. Cap. (Archbishop). *The Role of the Priest in Public Affairs*. First Things, August 30, 2008.

Chautard, Jean-Baptiste OCSO. *The Soul of the Apostolate*. Charlotte, NC: TAN Books. 2008

Claude de la Colombiere, SJ (Saint) *Trustful Surrender to Divine Providence*. Rockford, IL: Tan Books and Publishers, Inc. 1983

Concepcion Cabrera de Armida (Venerable). *Holy Hours*. Staten Island, NY: Alba House. 2006

Costa, Anne. *Lord I Hurt! The Grace of Forgiveness & The Road to Healing*. Frederick, MD: The Word Among Us Press. 2012

Delbrel, Madeleine. *We, the Ordinary People of the Streets*. Grand Rapids, MI: Wm. Eerdmans Publishing Company. 2000

DiLorenzo. Marie. Translator Robert Ventresca *Blessed Pier Giorgio Frassati: An Ordinary Christian*.

Dubay, Thomas, S.M., *Fire Within-St Teresa of Avila, St. John of the Cross, and the Gospel on Prayer*. San Francisco CA: Ignatius Press. 1989

Dubriel, Michael. *The Power of the Cross-Applying the Passion of Christ to Your Life.* Huntington, IN: Our Sunday Visitor Inc. 2004

Ehler, Sidney Z. *Church and State Through the Ages.* Cheshire, CT: Biblo-Moser. 1988

Eudes, John (Saint) *The Life and Kingdom of Jesus in Christian Souls.* New York, NY: P.J. Kennedy & Sons. 1946

Eymard, Peter Julian (Saint) *How To Get More Out of Holy Communion.* Manchester, NH: Sophia Institute Press, 2000

Faber, Frederick. *The Precious Blood.* Philadelphia, PA: The Peter Reilly Company.1959

Fallible Blogma. *7 Steps to a Holier Life.* http://fallibleblogma.com/index.php/7-steps-to-a-holier-life-by-mother-teresa/

Farrell, Walter, OP, STM and Healy, Martin STD. *My Way of Life.* Brooklyn, NY: Confraternity of the Precious Blood. 1952

Fernandez, Francis, *In Conversation With God.* London, UK: Scepter. 2003

Ferrer, Vincent, O.P. *A Treatise on the Spiritual Life.* Washington, DC: Dominicana Publications. 1956

Gardiner, Harold C, SJ. *Edmund Campion-Hero of God's Underground.* New Delhi, India: Vision Books. 1992

Herbst, Winfrid, SDS. *The Way to God.* St. Nazianz, WI: Society of the Divine Savior. 1947. Out of print

Hinnesbusch, Paul. O.P. *The Real Presence. It Is So!* http://www.frpaulhinnebusch.org/html/archive.html

Marmion, Columba, O.S.B. (Blessed) *The Mysteries of the Rosary.* http://www.ewtn.com/library/Prayer/MYSTROSA.HTM

John of the Cross (Saint). Editor: E. Allison Peters. *Ascent of Mount Carmel.* Mineola, NY: Dover Publications. 2008

Martin, Ralph. Dr. *Will Many Be Saved? What Vatican II Actually Teaches and Its Implications for the New Evangelization.* Grand Rapids, MI: Wm B. Eerdmans Publishing Co. 2012

Menendez, Josefa. *The Way of Divine Love.* Rockford, IL: TAN Books and Publishers, Inc. 1981

Myers, Rawley. *Daily Readings in Catholic Classics*. San Francisco, CA: Ignatius Press. 1992

Newton, Joseph Fort. What Have *The Saints to Teach Us*. Grand Rapids, MI: Fleming H. Revell Company. 1914

Noffke, Suzanne, O.P. Translator. *The Letters of St. Catherine of Siena, Vol. I-IV*. Tempe, AZ: Medieval and Renaissance Texts and Studies, Arizona State University. 2000, 2001, 2007, 2008.

Paone, Anthony J., SJ. *My Daily Bread*. Brooklyn, NY: Confraternity of the Precious Blood. 1954

Pascal, Blaise. *Pensees*. http://www.gutenberg.org/ebooks/18269

Rudloff, Leo, O.S.B. *Everyman's Theology*. Fort Collins, CO: Roger A. McCaffrey Publishing. 1919

Schneider, Athanasius (Most Rev.). *Dominus Est- It Is The Lord!* Pine Beach, NJ: Newman House Press. 2008

Sheen, Fulton J. (Venerable). *Love Is Not Tolerance*. Bellevue, WA: Catholic Education Resource Center
http://www.catholiceducation.org/articles/apologetics/ap0014.html

Sheen, Fulton, J. (Venerable). Rad*icalism and Sacrifice*. New York, NY: Catholic Information Society, 1966. Out of print

Sheen, Fulton, J. (Venerable). *The Life of Christ*. Garden City, NY: Image Books. 1954

Sheen, Fulton, J. (Venerable). *The Priest Is Not His Own*. San Francisco, CA: Ignatius Press. 1963

Sheen, Fulton J. (Venerable) *Those Mysterious Priests*. Boston, MA: Society of St. Paul. 2005

Sheen, Fulton, J. (Venerable). *Through The Year with Fulton Sheen*. Ann Arbor, MI: Servant Publications. 1985

Teresa of Avala (Saint). *Book of Foundations*. Carmelite Book Studies.
http://carmelite-book-studies--foundations.blogspot.com/

Teresa of Avila (Saint). *The Interior Castle*. Charlotte, NC: Saint Benedict Press, LLC. 2010

Teresa of Avila (Saint). *The Way of Perfection*. New York, NY: Image Books. 1954

Vianney, John Marie (Saint) *Sermons of the Cure of Ars.* Long Praire, MN: The Neumann Press. 1901

About the Author

Michael Seagriff practiced law for 30 years, as a general practitioner, prosecutor, criminal defense attorney and Administrative Law Judge.

His vocation as a Lay Dominican created an insatiable desire to learn, study, live and share his Faith. For more ten years he led a Prison Ministry program and has spent more then twelve years promoting Perpetual Eucharistic Adoration, serving as coordinator of that devotion in his former parish. He always wanted to write and share these experiences but never seemed to have the time when he was working. All that changed unexpectedly in 2009 when he retired.

Articles that he has written since retiring have been published in *Homiletic & Pastoral Review*, *The Catholic Sun*, a weekly diocesan newspaper, and on *Catholic Exchange.com* *CatholicLane.com*, *Catholic Online.com*, *Catholic Writers Guild Blog*, and *Zenit.org*.

The author acquired his healthy sense of humor and his love for the Catholic Faith from his deceased Dad and Mom and employs both frequently, sometimes to the joy and at other times to the consternation of those closest to him.

He blogs at: http://harvestingthefruitsofcontemplation.blogspot.com/.

Other Books By Author

Forgotten Truths To Set Faith Afire! Words To Challenge, Inspire and Instruct

The Catholic Writers Guild awarded its Seal of Approval to *Forgotten Truths to Set Faith – Words To Challenge, Inspire and Instruct.*

This is a compilation of over 1200 essential but *Forgotten Truths* that opened the author's eyes, spoke to his heart and stirred his soul. The power of these words changed his life and can do the same for all read and reflect upon them.

Fleeting Glimpses of The Silly, Sentimental and Sublime

This book is a mini-memoir containing 20 of the author's personal memories and reflections that he hopes will bring you laughter at a time you feel forlorn, comfort when you are overburdened with the challenges of daily living, tears of joy when certain words you read or images they generate resurrect thoughts of those you loved and lost, greater appreciation for the gift of life, zeal for the salvation of your soul, and an increased desire to give to God and those He created what He and they deserve.

Copies of both books are available in soft cover and Kindle formats and can be purchased on Amazon.com

www.ingramcontent.com/pod-product-compliance
Lightning Source LLC
Chambersburg PA
CBHW060623030426
42337CB00018B/3169